Considering Development

of Humans

Psychological Development

Issues

By Thomas Hodge

Table of Contents

Adversity and Development

The article examines the connections between adversities that are claimed to be associated with lower socio-economic status and an individual's development. Blair and Raver (2012) begin by examining the connections between parenting styles associated with lower socio-economic status and the development of the child. The authors make explore the possibility that stresses caused by poverty detract from the ability of the parent to effectively perform in the parental role. This is seen as negatively impact the abilities of the parent which results in long-term short-term and long term costs for the child's health and development. The authors constitute such a claim by utilizing the experiential canalization model. This model provides explanations for the connections between adversities and the quality of caregiving that results in the production of stress hormones that affect the neural connectivity of the individual. As the individual develops, self-regulating process that are the product of such processes create self-regulating behaviors. These behaviors are adaptions that develop in the individual to adjust for the adversities that are experienced in an environment of poverty.

In attempting to provide for a solution to the developmental deficiencies of the impoverished individuals, the authors suggest that parents take part in parenting education classes to be trained on how to be parents. This process of retraining the parents would be accomplish through parental interventions in addition to the education. The authors also made mention of environmental conditions associated with the state of poverty coming from other elements of the situation but did not offer a prescribed solution to such contributing factors.

In relevant research, McBride-Murry et al. (2011) examined other contributing factors to the development of youths in low-income areas. In addition to parenting styles, they found that the community outside of the family as opposed to family reinforced many behaviors that can be seen as negatively affecting development. This article expands the focus from the parents to the community as a whole. Duncan, Ziol-Guest and Kalil (2010) conducted a correlational study of connections between parental income and several measures in regards to the child's mental state and development. They found a correlation between the level of distress in the child and the parent's income only after the child had reach school age. There was no significant correlation in younger children. In light of such research, one could see a dynamic between the adversities only affecting the child once they are exposed to social situations outside of the familial environment. Other factors of stress were not found to be significant until the child reach school age or adolescence in the study.

Blair and Raver (2012) have made several connections in their article that are held together by various stereotypes and biases. The authors' focus on the parenting styles of lower socio-economic status parents neglects other environmental variables and factors that could clearly be seen as impacting the development of the individual. The community in which the individual grew up in could be seen as a clear factor that would impact development. The community provides the individual with certain resource such as schools, exposure to cultural norms, and opportunities for implicit learning. Individuals in poverty typically live in neighborhoods and communities that are deficient in such resources to provide for the advancement of development in children. These resources are different from those that are provided by the parents.

In addition to the focus on parenting styles, the authors claim that stress negatively impacts the development of the child. The concept of stress can be healthy in certain circumstances. Stress affords the child an opportunity to adapt and adjust to new experiences. The child would become accustomed to stress in his or her environmental situation and would be capable of handling stressful situations later in life. There is truth to the claim that too much stress could have negative consequences, but the authors build their claims on indirect stress that results from the parenting styles of low-income families. This type of conclusion seems to confuse a correlation with causation and additionally provide for the advancement of a stereotyping of low-income families by means of over-generalization.

Attachment and Development

Dykas and Cassidy (2011) examined how that attachment styles between infants and mothers affect cognitive abilities of the child in later life. The article examined the connections between how attachment-related information is processed by individuals that experienced different types of attachment styles. The individuals who were secure-attachment types as infants were positively biased when processing information that was related to attachments. The infants that were insecure-avoidant attempted to avoid or ignore information that would be processed and associated with attachment. The insecure-disorganized infants similarly displayed behavior that was indifferent or confused when processing information that was associated with attachments.

The research on the attachment styles of parents toward the children revealed insights into how the children process information associated with social interactions throughout development. A correlation exists between the attachment style experienced by the child in infancy and biasing of information processing toward either negative or positive social information. The children with insecure experiences were more easily able to process negative information while secure experiences biased children toward easier processing of positive experiences. This connection between attachment and processing abilities demonstrates the impact that early parenting has on the cognitive functioning of children later in life. Such a connection demonstrates the impact of early experiences across the lifespan of an individual and the influence on the susceptibility of the individual to present anxious tendencies, avoidant tendencies, and the likelihood of giving cognitive preference to specific types of information over others.

Numerous other studies have examined the same concept that was explored by Dykas and Cassidy (2011). Von der Lippe, Eilertsen, Hartmann, and Killen (2010) found a similar connection between early parental attachment styles and children's sensitivity to learning information during tutoring sessions. O'Connor and McCartney (2007) found a correlation between insecure attachment types and testing abilities along with a decreased likelihood of environmental exploration in pre-school children. The connections made by other researchers reinforce the findings that were made by Dykas and Cassidy (2011). In addition to current research, one could also consider the support of classical theories such as the proposal by Erikson (1968) that during the time of early childhood, one develops an understanding of whether to trust or mistrust their environment. If the environment provides a bias toward mistrust, the individual would present a bias toward mistrusting environments and situations that could be generalized to scenarios with connections to similarities of early childhood. The maladaptive strategies developed during this time in early development would have a clear impact on the abilities of the child to mature and develop in later stages due to the biasing effect of prior experience in the child's infancy.

In examining Dykas and Cassidy (2011), the article could have taken a closer look at the concepts of defensive exclusions and schema-driven social information processing. The two concepts appear to have the potential for explaining an interesting dynamic in how individuals may develop certain perspectives and maintain different biases throughout life. The dynamic interaction between the two concepts has the possibility of being correlated to attentional biases, loss aversion, negativity biases, and number of other possible biases associated with tendencies of individuals to make less than accurate decisions based on past influences in life. The applications and testing of potential correlations between attachment-styles and cognitive functions and biases could be easily tested with simple questionnaires. Such correlations could be used to determine the likelihood of adolescents to develop particular schemas associated with the patterns of development seen in similar individuals with the same attachment-style parent. This could be used in developing treatment plans or training to assist the individuals with finding improved ways of coping with emotional biases that they have or, at least, being aware of the biases and sources of such biases.

The early identification of school age or preschool age children as being socialized in the specific attachment-style environments would provide educators with a better understanding of the causes of such cognitive deficits. Treating the cognitive deficit in the absence of understanding the contributing factors serves to only redirect developmental problems to reoccur at a different instance or opportunity. To understand the cause the cognitive deficit can provide directed and specific plans in restructuring the individual's understanding and mindset of their environment. Once the mindset of the child is addressed, the child will be able to produce long-term improvements in cognitive functioning. This would be an applicable direction for this research to develop into with the hope of improving the quality of development, education, and life of individuals.

Attention Deficit Hyperactivity Disorder

Marchetta, Hurks, Krabbendam, and Jolles (2008) examined the differences in cognitive functioning between adults with ADHD that was co-morbidly present with another condition, adults with ADHD independent of comorbidity, adults with some symptoms but not diagnosable with ADHD, and adults that were free of ADHD symptoms. Marchetta et al. (2008) explored four different executive functions and two non-executive functions. The executive functions were interference control, concept shifting, verbal fluency, and verbal working memory. The non-executive functions were attention capacity and information processing functions. The researchers used a variety of assessments such as Stroop Task, Trail Making Test, and Verbal Fluency Test to measure differences in functioning among the different groups of the specific cognitive functions.

Marchetta et al. (2008) found deficits for the group that was co-morbidly diagnosed with ADHD and another disorder and the group with ADHD symptoms but not the disorder on both non-cognitive tasks that can attribute the deficits in those areas to variables other than ADHD. The ADHD groups showed no deficits in verbal fluency or interference control, but deficits were present in the ADHD groups in the areas of verbal working memory and concept shifting. Such findings demonstrate that a unique way in which ADHD affects specific aspects of cognitive functioning as opposed to cognitive functioning general. In narrowing down the specific impact of ADHD on an individual's functioning, improved methods of training and adaptation of educational systems can be implemented to improve the functioning of individuals that suffer from ADHD.

Gupta and Kar (2010) examined how the differences in specific cognitive tasks can be used to more accurately differentiate between ADHD and other diagnoses that have similar symptoms to ADHD. This research attempted to address the similar issue of how ADHD can be discriminated from other disorders such as mood disorders, behavior disorders, and developmental disorders for the purpose of providing the individuals with appropriate treatment that will produce effective results. Gupta and Kar (2010) took the compared the psychometric properties of a variety of assessment tools such as the Gordon Diagnostic System, Test of Variables of Attention, Conner's Continuous Performance Task, and IVA to determine how the assessments would be able to focus on the specific cognitive deficits associated with ADHD. The research also examined how effective the assessments were at discriminating the specific deficits from associated with ADHD from other comorbid conditions that are common to co-occur with ADHD.

Examining such assessment tools along with the reliability and validity of parent and teacher reporting could be used to explain the high rates of comorbidity of ADHD being coupled with other diagnoses. One can note that a misdiagnosis of an individual could result in severe consequences that could lead to a worsening of the condition that the individual is experiencing. Waite and Ramsey (2010) described how that many individuals were undiagnosed as children with ADHD due to limitations on resources but the signs of ADHD were present for them during adulthood and created a great deal of hardships during adolescences and adulthood. The individuals in the study were diagnosed incorrectly defined as not having

ADHD during youth or were diagnosed as having a disorder that presented similar symptoms. Through further research into the specific effects of ADHD on cognitive functions, better diagnostic measures and improved treatment plans can be defined for individuals that suffer from ADHD.

The shortcoming of Marchetta et al. (2008) was that the ADHD was compared against such a wide array of disorders that were not controlled for specific disorders. The information is helpful in determining what areas could be easily confused between ADHD and other disorders in general; however, a more useful approach would be to develop a series of studies to define how each specific disorder could be confused with ADHD. Since ADHD seems to have a history of over-representation in certain areas, such a series of studies could be condensed into useful literature to aid clinicians in improving the accuracy of their diagnoses with regard to ADHD and other disorders that develop in early childhood. Additionally, such research could be presented in simpler to advance the understanding of educators, social workers, and family members allowing them to develop a clearer understanding of such disorders and the necessary treatments for the specific cases based on the underlying maladaptive processes that lead to such conditions as ADHD or its co-morbid conditions that are often confused with ADHD.

Attentional Control and Aging

Waszak, Hommel, and Shu-Chen (2010) examined the development of the processes of orienting and conflict resolution as they regard to attentional control. The research attempted to compare and contrast the development of the two processes across lifespan development by measuring the reaction times of the individuals on the Posner-type orienting task and the Eriksen-type flanker task. The research revealed that individuals developed much younger in the orienting task than the conflict resolution task. The individuals performed the orienting task at their adult-like levels by age ten to eleven years of age while the conflict resolution task did not achieve their adult-like levels until around fifteen years of age.

Waszak, Hommel and Shu-Chen (2010) demonstrate how the simpler cognitive ability of orienting in attentional control matures much earlier than a more complex function such as conflict resolution. These findings correlate with the development patterns of higher functioning regions of the brain such as the development of prefrontal regions of the brain that are responsible for higher levels of thought such as planning and executive functions. The research shows that the tasks also show a decline with aging into later adulthood. The orienting task shows a much slower decline than the conflict resolution task shows as the individuals mature into later adulthood. This type of differential decline between the two functions can be seen as a demonstration of how more advanced functions deteriorate more rapidly than less advanced functions. Cognitive functions that develop earlier in life are retained longer than the functions that develop later in life.

In a similar study, Castel et al. (2011) examined how the processes of recall and selectivity of encoding information based on importance. In the task, individuals were to attempt to encode and recall items from a list. The items were given varying values based on their importance that was explained to the individuals that higher value items would be worth more points. One can note that encoding and recall of items is less cognitively complex than ascribing values to the items for the purpose of balancing mental effort and giving preference to encoding the higher value items. The recall ability was noted as developing earlier in age to peak performance than selectivity. In contrast to the study of Waszak, Hommel, and Shu-Chen (2010), the more complex task of selectivity continued to maintain its higher levels of performance into older ages. The selectivity ability did not begin to decline until very late in life. The recall ability began to a gradual decline in middle-aged adults. In light of such research, one can note that cognitive ability differs in decline due to more than the determination of the simplicity and complexity or the age of acquiring the skill. Selectivity can be noted as being vastly more complex than the recall ability, but the selectivity performance maintains much longer than the recall of the individual.

To make sense of this contradiction, one must adjust the theory of earlier acquired skills lasting for longer durations of time as declared by Waszak, Hommel, and Shu-Chen (2010). The shortcoming in both studies is that each study is only comparing two cognitive abilities. Due to this type of design, the authors can be led to make an overgeneralizing statement concerning the development and longevity of cognitive process across the life span of an individual. Theoretically, such a statement can be easily disputed due to the possibility of further research that could challenge the theory by comparing two separate cognitive processes across lifespan development. Multiple cognitive functions could be compared by means of ANOVA to determine if earlier a cognitive process develops impacts the retention of such processes through older age. In further examining such correlations, a variety of other variables could be explored such as rehearsal of the particular cognitive ability over the lifetime, utilization of cognitive ability during the particular time in life, the importance of the function as it relates to the individual's current phase in life, and various other factors. These factors could be taken into consideration as to how they affect the cognitive decline of particular functions in later life and allow

for a fuller explanation of the relevance of
how earlier mastery of cognitive functions
can play a role in the retention of such
functions into elderly phases of life.

Cognitive Development

The development of an individual varies dependent on the type of cognitive function that is being examined based on the study of Cuevas and Bell (2010). In their research, the development of a child is examined by comparing response times in relation to reaching for a desired object as opposed to looking in the direction of the desired object. The study examines how the infant reacts utilizing the application of object permanence tests and timing the reaction time of the response of the child. The research notes that the child progresses through the ages of five months to ten months of age to have quicker response times. The researchers also examined differences of how the reversal of tasks affects the performance of the infant by comparing the reaction times of infants who performed reaching tasks first as opposed to those who performed the looking tasks first. The research displayed how early trials of the test showed improved better performance in the looking trials than the reaching trials. In the later trials, the infants improved more rapidly regarding the reaching task to where it began to surpass the looking task response times.

Similarly, Watanabe et al. (2012) used the A-not-B task to measure changes in the development of attention capabilities of infants between ten to twelve months in age by comparing the response times in a longitudinal study and by comparing also the effects of a distractor in the reaction times of the infants. Watanabe et al. (2012) found that the response times of the infants were more affected by the distractor at age ten months, but the twelve-month-old infants showed no difference in response times as compared to the infants of the same age without a distractor. Through this research, Watanabe et al. (2012) was able to demonstrate how rapid attention functions develop at this point in the life of the child. Matthews and Ellis (1996) performed a similar study to examine the developmental differences between infants that were delivered at full term and infants born prematurely. In doing so, Matthews, Ellis, and Nelson (1996) found that the preterm infants showed quicker response times but a greater number of errors than the full term children. Notably, both groups showed improvements at the same ages regardless of whether they were preterm or full term infants. As age progressed, the differences became less noticeable in error rate and reaction times in the study.

Cuevas and Bell (2010) noted that difference within groups was present in their study, as they had controlled for numerous factors such as whether infants were born premature or full term, socioeconomic status, and allowed for the participants to come from varying ethnic backgrounds. A factor that seems to have been overlooked was variance in parenting styles. One can always note that differences occur because life does not occur in a vacuum. Individual differences exist due to such potential factors as situational differences and experiences between infants. One could examine differences on a wide range of variables to determine differences. Regardless of the variables, the research does show the particular changes in reaction times at specific points in development. The times that reaction times improve notably could serve as potential milestones in cognitive development. With a large enough sample size, one could construct potential models of the development of various cognitive functions that would serve to determine the developmental tendencies of individual infants. To allow such models to serve as predictors of development at such a young age has latent negative consequences to consider. Inadequately trained individuals could misuse such a predictive model and allow for the generalization of such a test. With great caution, such a model and associated testing procedures could be used to determine what appropriate stimuli and interaction would best serve the development of a young child in his or her cognitive development through the early stages of development.

Cultural Impact on Development

Chen (2012) explored the impacts of cultural influences on the development of children as they interacted with their peers. The differences appeared in the context of whether the culture that the children originated from was individualistic or collectivist in nature. The individualistic cultures promoted characteristics of assertiveness and aggressiveness in the children. These types of behaviors could be seen as having connections to the culture's emphasis on the success of the individual and the advancement of competitiveness. Conversely, the collectivist cultures promoted the characteristics of self-discipline and conformity among the children. Due to this, the children that were seen as being quite and reserved were more accepted by their peers as opposed to those of similar characteristics in individualistic cultures. The peer groups in the individualistic cultures rejected the quite children and accepted the aggressive and assertive children in a contrary manner to what would have occurred in a collectivist culture among the children. In using this example, Chen (2012) points out how the society influence the social interactions of children which then serves to perpetuate societal norms of what is social accepted and rewarded behavior.

Diesendruck and Markson (2011)

examined how that the culture in which a child develops aids in providing the child with a schema system to identify what is normal and what is expected. Schema theory is often associated with learning during early development. As the child notices the interactions and similarities between individuals and their behaviors, the child is provided with more details as to how he or she should understand each category of people to behave. The behaviors are divided into what is considered adult behavior and kid behavior. As the child-peer groups develop, the children learn from the interpersonal relations of those around them how to form peer groups. Culture plays a part by providing consistency in the interactions of adults and older children that have developed their peer groups based on what they had observed. Observing a single instance of how a group of individuals behaves, treats its members, and accepts and rejects individuals would have a diminished impact on how a child forms a schema of how a peer group should function. The consistency of observed peer groups having the same behaviors, rules, and norms of interaction strengthens the schema that the child has developed about peer groups. Other children in the same culture have made the same observations of peer interactions because the other children are seeing very similar interactions. This consistency in interaction between observed groups is the product of culture. In this manner, one can see how the culture plays a strong part in defining early in development what peer interactions should consist of and continuing to reinforce and strengthen that idea over time through consistent reiteration of the originally developed schemas.

The shortcoming of Chen (2012) is his concept of rewarding shyness as being reinforcement for the quality. If one considers the logic of this concept, the idea seems self-defeating. First, the author should have defined shyness in at least an operational manner. If shyness were to be a desire to avoid attention, the social rewarding of shyness would be counter-productive to continue the quality. This concept should have been explained in greater detail for the article to have a strong stance. The quality of shyness does seem to be a common quality that is displayed among individuals of many eastern cultures; however, the influencing that behavior by peer-interactions does not seem like a strong enough connection to fully explain the development of that particular quality. There are some collectivist cultures in which shyness is not a pronounced quality. The author may have neglected possible third variables for that quality being displayed in traditional Asian cultures. Chen's (2012) mention of social development as an active process seems to be an idea that should be further evaluated. As social development would be an active process, this concept would present an opportunity for change to be made to social process development through activity changes and modifications to the interactions that the culture has provided for the development of what children should find socially acceptable and expected. With a better understanding of how the social development is active, one could develop methods by which to change cultural problems such as stereotyping, racism, bullying, and other various social behaviors.

Developmental Psychopathology

Lorber and Egeland (2009) examined the relationship between poor-quality parenting during infancy and the externalization of psychopathology at various ages in development. The researchers measured the quality of parenting at the ages of three months and six months. They, then, measured the externalizing behaviors of the children based on parental report in kindergarten, first grade, and age 16. The tracking of the behaviors continued into adulthood through self-report from the individuals at ages 16, 23, and 26. Lorber and Egeland (2009) found that there was a correlation between the parent styles and the behaviors at the younger ages. The relationship disappeared during adolescence and then reappeared in adulthood.

The authors explain that the decrease in correlation between the quality of parenting during infancy and psychopathology during adolescence can be explained by environmental factors. They found that the correlations in early childhood and adulthood could be the result of the same mechanisms affecting behavioral presentations in the individuals. The mechanisms that affected the behaviors included modeling, genetics, and control. During adolescence, the researchers found that the environmental stimuli associated with that period of development were influential enough to overcome the influence of the poor parenting that was experienced during infancy.

Psychogiou, Daley, Thompson, and Sonuga-Barke (2008) found that improved parenting-styles foster higher levels of empathy in the parents. These higher levels of empathy reduced the externalizing of psychopathology in adolescences. When considering this research, one might consider how the parenting styles may have changed since infancy. If some of the parents had improved their parenting styles over time and other would not have, the effects on the presentation of psychopathology during adolescence would have been affected unevenly. McKinney and

Milone (2012) examined how parenting and the psychopathology of the parent affected the psychopathology of individuals in adolescence. They found that the effects varied based on whether the negative parenting or psychopathology was related to the mother or father. They found that negative parenting was directly related to late-adolescence psychopathology when it was related to the mother, but an inverse relationship occurred when it was related to the father. In consideration of the variable of maternal or parental parenting, one may consider the effect to be better understood if the differences were examined in the study of Lorber and Egeland (2009).

Lorber and Egeland (2009) fails to fully address the possible difference between subjects during the adolescence period. There exists a high degree of variation that could be used to account for the lack of correlation that existed during the adolescence period. Additionally, the gaps in time between measures lessens the strength of accuracy in the explanations of how the patterns of externalizing psychopathology occurs. The first two measures of externalizing behaviors were a year apart. From the second measure to the third measurement, a period of ten years was unexamined. The study would have provided a much better explanation of the relationships if the measures were done in a more consistent manner. The behaviors that were measured would have produced some skewed representations across the age groups. The factors that were compiled to provide the measures of externalizing behaviors could have also been examined independently to determine if certain types of behaviors were more influenced than others.

The reasons that were provided for the dip in correlation during adolescence could have been more attentive to the psychosocial development that occurs during adolescence. If one were to consider the degree of typical rebellious behavior that occurs during adolescence, one could consider some individuals to be exhibiting rebellious behavior in the form of rebelling against what they had grew to know as a norm in early childhood. The rebellion of adolescence could be used to more accurately explain this dip while the conforming of more individuals to their perceived social norms during adulthood could be used to explain their return to the correlation. Some individuals would embrace the new norms of behavior based on what they had learned during their rebellious adolescences resulting in the small effect size in adulthood than early childhood.

Dynamic Systems Model

The dynamic systems model serves as a proposed model of human development that attempts to two major development concepts. The first concept is Piaget's idea of accommodation and assimilation, and the second concept is Vygotsky's concept of proximal zone and actual development. van Geert (1998) attempted to show that the interaction between the ideas produced a dynamic interaction that could be seen to predict the development of an individual. Piagetian development models are often noted as being stage models in which development is seen to be discontinuous as it progresses in a jumping manner from one stage to the next. Models based on Vygogsky's concept of a proximal zone of development are often viewed as a continuous development that progresses over time without the sudden jumps that are seen in the Piagetian models. The dynamic systems model attempts to show that the development is shown to progress through a series of fluctuations that provide an advancement of the individual from an earlier mode of thought to a more advanced mode of thought in a manner that is not linear but oscillatory.

To explain such oscillations through the development of the individual, one can note the effect of help upon the individual's progression and the absence of the help as being the downward oscillation. Since an individual's development in an upward manner, these oscillations tend to still advance the individual in an upward fashion but in a function that appears as an S-shaped curve as opposed to a linear curve. The oscillatory nature of the development curve also accounts for the appearance of stages or plateaus in the individual's development.

In examining recent literature that addresses the proposal put forth in the article, research in to the development of language and reading skills stands out as a major application in which such a model could be tested. Hohenberger and Peltzer-Karpf (2009) examined language development utilizing the dynamic systems model of development to find a similar S-shaped function present in the development of language acquisition that reflected a combination of nature and nurture as van Geert (1998) predicted concerning the dynamic model of development. Lynch et al. (2008) examined the development of early reading comprehension in children to find that the interactions between the different skills required for reading comprehension development produced a similar pattern to the proposed function seen in the dynamic systems model of development.

The relationship between the article and current research in to language development and reading comprehension would seem to be clearly related in the pattern of developmental advancement of the individuals. In addition to the functional pattern, one can also note that the current research shows that not only is the pattern similar but also the interactions among variables is a clear connection between existing literature and van Geert's (1998) proposal of the dynamic systems model. This connection represents the bridge between the concepts presented by Piaget and Vygotsky to provide a more encompassing view of human development. The dynamics model laid groundwork for future models of development as can be seen in the related literature.

The dynamic systems model serves as a superb outline of how development occurs in a vacuum when a specific element of development can be separated from third variables. Unfortunately, the downfall of the study is that development does not occur in a vacuum. The possibility of separating each individual variable from all other elements of the environment is appealing but not feasible. A grand model that fully takes into account all variables that affect how an individual develops would be a continuously changing model that would always contain flaws due to the ever-changing environment that affects the individuals who develop. Geert (1998) claims that the dynamic model that is presented in the article would only be a starting point that could be modified by future research. By attempting to develop a grand model of development, the model would be ethnocentric in nature because it would only address the development of a particular group while ignoring the differences of other group's development that would be different such as differences in culture, gender, and individual experiences. Due to the issues with sampling, the group from which the information would be obtain would need to be more diverse and representative of humanity than the group used. Once these shortcomings are addressed, such a model could have the potential to explain some of how development occurs or provide insight into differences in development between individuals or groups of individuals.

PARENTING

Belsky, Steinberg, Houts, and Halpern-Felsher (2010) examined the connection between maternal harshness and early menarche. Early menarche has been associated with an increase in sexual risk-taking behaviors. The research attempted to support BSD theory of paternal absence being associated with increased sexual behaviors leading to pregnancy at an earlier age as a reproductive strategy of natural selection. The study utilized a longitudinal method of observation to make the relation between parenting styles of the mother and sexual risk-taking behavior by having the mothers complete a questionnaire when the child was four years old and following up with the child until the age of fifteen to evaluate sexual behaviors. The researchers adjusted the age of menarche to take into account hereditary effects. Belsky et al. (2010) found a correlation between the harshness of the mother's parenting style and the age of menarche after taking into account heredity factors. A stronger connection existed between the age of menarche and risk-taking of both a sexual nature and other risk-taking behaviors. A strong correlation also occurred between the parental harshness and other risk-taking behaviors. Belsky et al. (2010) explained that the relationships that exist between the variables strengthen the BSD theory that the absence of a father leads to earlier sexual behaviors due to reproductive strategies.

Harden and Mendle (2012) examined whether the environment has an impact on the onset of menarche in girls. As expected, they found that the environment does have an impact on the time of menarche onset. Wierson, Long, and Forehand (1993) examined the affects of familial stress upon the age of menarche onset to determine that girls in stress situations experienced earlier menarche than those not in stressful situations. Mendle, Leve, Van Ryzin, Natsuaki, and Ge (2011) examined the correlations of abuse and mistreatment to the age of menarche onset to find that abuse and mistreatment had a strong correlation to the age of menarche onset in young girls. The connection that each of these studies have is that girls that experience greater degrees of stress experience an earlier menarche that those who experience less stress. Aegidius et al. (2011) explained that the hormones of estrogen and progesterone play a keep part in menstrual cycles and also react to stress. The connection between hormones associated with menarche and stress could more accurately explain the connections between the earlier onset of menarche and situations that would produce more stress during the life of a young girl.

Belsky et al. (2010) has a great number of flaws in their support of BSD theory. The research presented in Belsky et al. (2010) attempts to misattribute causation to correlation. The connections that were made were between the factors of parental harshness and early menarche were correlational as the observations were naturalistic and not a true experiment that could be manipulated to explain causation. In addition to the correlation-causation error, the connection between parental harshness and the absence of a father seems to be an irrational connection. The absence or presence of a father would seem to be unconnected to the degree of harshness that a girl experiences.

BSD theory contains its own theoretical flaws. BSD theory attributes earlier menarche to reproductive strategies as a result of natural selection to increase the likelihood of reproduction and continuation of the species. If this were the case, one would be able to notice a decrease in the age of menarche over time as it would be a trait that would advance the continuation of the species. Additionally, the earlier menarche would be seen as beneficial to the species. As the individual would reach menarche earlier and reproduce earlier by theory, the offspring would not be provided for properly and have a reduced chance of survival due to the immaturity of the mother.

The connection that can be made between the absence of a father and parental harshness is that of the level of stress that is experienced by the child. Stress levels seem to be a reoccurring factor among the studies of menarche determinants. The connections between risk-taking behavior and early menarche could be attributed to hormonal changes that could be examined by a detailed study of the bio-chemical changes that occur as a result of menarche. It would have been more interesting to see if there was more a connection between parental harshness and sexual risk taking if the age of menarche was controlled for as opposed to be a variable that was not adjusted for in the correlations present by Belsky et al. (2010). The connections between harshness and sexual behaviors would serve to explain that connection more directly if one were to conduct further research to determine the occurrences of risk-taking behaviors when menarche is statistically controlled for among participants to determine the impact of parental harshness upon risk-taking behaviors directly.

Peer Influence on Development

Garandeau, Ahn, and Rodkin (2011) examined the relationships between the hierarchical structure of classrooms and emphasis on academic performance to aggressiveness of individuals in the classrooms. The study focused on fourth and fifth grade students in particular. The researchers found that the degree of difference between popular and unpopular students correlated with the degree of aggressiveness among the students. They found that schools where academic performance was emphasized more heavily were the schools were the aggressive students were also less popular. The study provided insight into potential strategies that could be used to decrease bullying and aggressive behavior in schools.

Garandeau et al. (2011) provided two explanations to how popular children were more aggressive than unpopular children. First, popular children would use aggressive behaviors to create a larger gap in status between them and less popular children. This gap would serve to elevate their social status in the classroom. The second explanation was that popular children had more to lose than unpopular children in the classrooms with a more structured hierarchical social structure. Due to this potential for loss, the popular children would display more aggressive behaviors in order to maintain their status of being popular.

Shi and Xie (2012) found that higher status members of groups among seventh graders were found to be more aggressive than other members of their groups. Additionally, the groups that had higher levels of aggression among the more popular individuals also showed increased levels of aggression among the members. Shi and Xie (2012) claim that the aggressiveness of high status individuals may also influence and impact the levels of aggression among the members. They found similar effects among both boys and girls in regards to social aggression. Among the male groups, they found a similar effect for levels of physical aggression in addition to the social aggression. As an individual's status level was lower, they found that the individual was less likely to be influenced by the aggressiveness of the higher-level members of the group on levels of aggression.

Mayeux and Cillessen (2008) examined changes in aggressiveness over the course of grades nine to twelve in relationship to the popularity of the individual and their awareness of their popularity. They found that popular individuals who knew they were popular developed higher levels of overt aggression over the course of high school than other groups. As a response to being disliked, students who knew they were disliked showed increase levels of relational aggression than other groups. The popular individuals can be seen as being overtly aggressive to maintain their standing, and disliked individuals can be seen to show relational aggression as a means of increasing their standing with others.

Grandeau, Ahn, and Rodkin (2011) make the error of explaining causation with a correlation. The article refers to the factors as being moderators of aggressive behaviors. Unfortunately, the research does not determine if the aggressive behaviors produced the other factors or if the other factors lead to the aggressive behaviors. One could hope that increasing interest in academic achievement would create lower levels of aggression and that a less hierarchical social system among children would lead to lower levels of aggression.

The issue is that increasing interest in academic achievement may simply reformulate a different structure of aggressive tendencies by simply redesigning a new social structure. The children would be smarter and study harder, but they would still be aggressive toward other children only in a more intelligent manner. The article proposed that by understanding the moderators of aggression one could control decrease the levels of bullying in schools and other similar behaviors. By mistaking correlation for causation, the true cause of such aggression may be overlooked and not addressed. If one were able to modify the structure of a fourth or fifth grade classroom to change the emphasis on academic achievement among the children, one would truly need to pay attention to the aggressive tendencies and the hierarchy of the classroom to see if the aggressive behaviors had decreased or simply been reassigned and redirected to fit the new structure.

A more effective way to examine the impact hierarchical structure of a classroom would impact aggressiveness would be to change the sizes of the classroom. Larger numbers of students may tend to develop a more structured hierarchy of popular and unpopular students with greater degrees of variation than smaller classes. If the children were changed between large and small class sizes, one could more effectively measure these variables but would still need to control for other factors. To design the experiment in this manner would have the potential for control of such factors if a correlation could be found and manipulated using an ABAB design for the experiment with counterbalancing measures across different groups.

School Readiness

Razza, Martin, and Brooks-Gunn (2010) examined the effects of specific environmental factors on the development of sustained attention and school readiness of children among low-income and middle class families. The study was designed to examine of parenting styles, environmental stimuli, and various factors associated with the child's home environment. The children were evaluated at age three for the degree to which the specific environmental factors were present. At age five, the children were evaluated to determine the child's level of school readiness. The results were compared to find correlations between the environmental factors and the child's development of cognitive abilities by the age of five.

Razza et al. (2010) found that the poor children scored lower on tasks that required focused attention and a lack of impulse control among the poor children. The research found connections between maternal hostility and the child's abilities to focus attention. The research describes the parent's lack of concern for the child's emotions and experience as being a contributory factor in the child's inability to focus during school due to the levels of anxiety in the child and devaluing of the child's understanding. Razza et al. (2010) also bring attention to the connect between the poor children's lack of being read to as opposed to the higher socioeconomic level children to which books are read. This connection increases the level of difficulty the children have with performing tasks that involve inhibiting impulses and focusing attention toward an activity of low levels of physical activity.

Doyle, McEntree, and McNamara (2012) examined the correlations between several common factors of low-income households and several factors of school readiness. In the study, the factors related to school readiness included not only cognitive factors related to academic skills but also social skills that may have had an impact on how the children would perform on such cognitive tasks. Among the factors, a significant relationship was found between the child's emotional maturity, which related to aggressiveness, pro-social behavior, anxiety coping skills, and attentiveness, and the parent's level of education. The connection between the two elements could have a connection to the child modeling the observed behavior of the parent in expressing emotions. Assuming that the higher level of education would result in improved verbal skills on the part of the parent, the child would be able to learn coping skills and expressive skills with regard to emotional control and maturity through observational learning.

In comparing Doyle et al. (2012) to Razza et al. (2012), one can note that measures of emotional maturity could possibly account for the child's lack of ability to focus. The maternal hostility could also be seen as modeling inappropriate emotional maturity of the child. In combining the findings of both studies, one could determine that parents of lower educational backgrounds could be less expressive of their emotions in a constructive manner. The maladaptive expression or lack of expression of emotions could be counterproductive in allowing the child to emotionally develop coping skills with regard to emotions and verbal skills as a result of less interaction through observational learning in the home environment that is afforded to better performing children.

The shortcoming with the study by Razza et al. (2012) is the assumption that inadequate parenting techniques and skills differ based on socioeconomic class. This assumption seems to be naïve and discriminatory based on class. A state of poverty may have the potential amplify the impacts of inadequate parenting techniques, or class difference may simply produce deficits in a different manner based on the availability of resources to individuals of differing social classes. In redesigning such a study using socioeconomic class as a variable, one attempt to observe the different ways in which children manifest shortcomings in school readiness factors among different socioeconomic classes. For example, a poor child may be hyperactive in pre-school while a wealthier child may be more aggressive. Correlations could examine a large number of contributing factors that may contribute to the differing manifestations as a result of poor parenting abilities across socioeconomic classes.

Additionally, the methods that were used in the study appeared to have their own shortcomings. The measures that were used by the researchers appeared to be very narrow in scope by using dichotomous questions that were limited in number. With such limited instruments, floor effects and ceiling effects should be expected to abound throughout the study since there were only eight possible scores on one of the measures. In addition to the measuring devices, Razzza et al. (2012) defined near-poor as being between 100% to 300% of the poverty guidelines. This range is rather extreme in nature as four-person household could make

between $23,050 and $69,150 per year
(United States Department of Health and
Human Services, 2012). With such a wide
range of income, the title of near-poor seems
to be a misrepresentation of the group to be
studied.

Intergenerational Trauma

Kaitz, M., Levy, M., Ebstein, R., Faraone, S. V., & Mankuta, D. (2009). The intergenerational effects of trauma from terror: A real possibility. *Infant Mental Health Journal, 30*(2), 158-179.

Kaitz et al. (2009) examined the effect of intergenerational trauma through terror (ITTT). The researchers provided several examples of how severe trauma effects children through the mannerisms of the parents. Kaitz et al. (2009) found that anxiety and depression that resulted from the trauma produced discord that manifested in the responses of the parent to the child, mistimed and lack of appraisal, and criticism control on the part of the parent. Since the parent would have pronounced difficulty maintaining their own emotional responses, social interactions between the parent and child would have been marked by hindrances to adequate interactions as would be typically expected in most parent-child dyads. As the relationship was affected by the trauma, the attachment between parent and child became very insecure due to the inadequate responses from the parent toward the child's needs, fears, and frustrations.

The authors proposed that the trauma would affect not only the relationship between parent and child but also biologically impact the child. The mothers who experienced PTSD symptoms during pregnancy had significantly lower levels of cortisol. The lower levels of cortisol are often associated with anxiety disorders and have an impact on the HPA-axis. While in prenatal stages of development, the child is provided with significantly lower than usually levels of cortisol that produces an impact on the infant's regulation of the HPA-axis. The HPA-axis plays a key role in metabolism, memory, and immunity. When cortisol levels are too high or low, the HPA-axis is affected by the imbalance of the cortisol. As the authors mention such a biological impact, they emphasis the impacts of ITTT through both biological and environmental factors.

Frankish, T., & Bradbury, J. (2012). Telling stories for the next generation: Trauma and nostalgia. Peace And Conflict: *Journal Of Peace Psychology, 18*(3), 294-306. doi:10.1037/a0029070

Frankish and Bradbury (2012) examined the intergenerational transmission of trauma as a result of apartheid in South Africa. Through their research, the researchers found that silence about the trauma between family members and nostalgia contributed to the effects of the trauma. Nostalgia served to define to the younger generations how life was so drastically changed by the events of the apartheid. Grandparents tell stories to grandchildren about how much better life was before the traumatic event and reflect that things were never the same after. Since all the children know is what life is like after the trauma, they assume a role of individuals that were directly affected by the traumatic events even though they never personally experienced the events.

Frankish and Bradbury (2012) noted that younger generations responded to the older generations when discussing the trauma of the apartheid as if they experienced the events themselves also. The best example was given when one of the children of an apartheid survivor answered questions about the survivor asked about events that occurred during apartheid, which happened before the younger individual was born. The traumatic events were discussed among family members rarely. The scarcity of the stories of trauma enriches the stories with a sense of novelty. The elders mentioned the stories only a few times to the younger generation so that the silence between the times that it is discussed strengthens the traumatic events and provides a connection for the younger generation to the events. The younger generation is often referred to as a "hinge" generation that is not yet free from the effects of the trauma but still a step toward making the trauma a notable history of their culture.

The article serves to show how storytelling between generations serves to provide a tie between the recent generations and the current generation so that the scars of a specific trauma carry on through history. This shows how that intergenerational transmission serves to display how severe a traumatic occurrence is based upon how relevant the experience feels for proceeding generations. The effect of the trauma can be seen also by the way that younger generations also see the trauma as separating them from the nostalgia of the past that is magnified by silence.

Baranowsky, A. B., Young, M., Johnson-Douglas, S., Williams-Keeler, L., & McCarrey, M. (1998). PTSD transmission: A review of secondary traumatization in Holocaust survivor families. *Canadian Psychology,*

39(4), 247-256.

doi:10.1037/h0086816

Baranowsky et al. (1998) explored how the children of holocaust survivors presented PTSD-like symptoms even though they had never experienced trauma. In the research, the children were found to be hyper-vigilant and untrusting of others. The children also report that they felt different from their peers and realized that they acted differently also. The research did address that the populations that were looked at were clinical populations that had came to the attention of mental health professionals by self-referral. Additionally, due to the nature of the holocaust, random sampling would be impossibility preventing a true experiment.

Baranowsky et al. (1998) addresses a variety of theories that has been used to explain the appearance of the symptoms in subsequent generations. The secondary PTSD could be explained as a symptom of deep understanding of the following generation about the prior generation in an attempt to understand their parents' struggles during the World War II era. The symptoms were also explored as being the product of storytelling compounded by silent periods. An evolutionary approach to the behaviors poses that the symptoms serve to be the younger generations reaction to the parents' attempts at teaching their children how to survive in times of persecution. This could be seen as an explanation based the concept of individuals' attempting to aid their genes in being based on through time. To promote the chances of lineage continuation, the survivors of the older generation develop attachment-styles and behave in ways that aide their children's survival based on the experiences of their lives when they were younger.

The author proposes that the transmission of trauma between generations could serve to set the expectations of clinicians treating PTSD sufferers. In light of such research, one should also look for symptoms of intergenerational transmission in the children of clients suffering from PTSD. The research does not provide a likelihood of transmission due to the claimed impossibility of designing such an experiment.

Field, N. P., Om, C., Kim, T., & Vorn, S. (2011). Parental styles in second generation effects of genocide stemming from the Khmer Rouge regime in Cambodia. *Attachment & Human Development, 13*(6), 611-628. doi:10.1080/14616734.2011.609015

Field et al. (2011) examined the effects of trauma due to trauma experienced during the Khmer Rouge genocide in Cambodia upon the parenting styles of survivors and the effects upon the proceeding generation. The researchers examined how attachment styles correlated with the trauma experienced by the parents and the anxiety and depression symptoms that were displayed in the children. The researchers found that the parents displayed a role reversal in the style of attachment. Typically, a child will look to a parent for emotional support. In the case of the Khmer Rouge survivors, the trauma of the parents reversed this interaction to where the parents began to look to the children as a source of emotional support in dealing with the parents' own past trauma.

The parents' traumatic experience served to provide a direct correlation with the children's levels of anxiety. The increased levels of anxiety could be seen as the result of the children having to cope with not only the stresses of growing up but also the stresses that resulted from being looked to for emotional support by the parent who was coping with PTSD from past events. The research also found a correlation between the trauma symptoms and the over-protectiveness of the maternal parent. The correlations of trauma to both role reversal and over-protectiveness serve to show two changes to parenting styles that are connected to traumatic experiences. Over-protectiveness and role reversals serve as the vehicle of transmission in the cases of anxiety and depression symptoms being transferred across generations as the result of events that were experienced by the parent.

Field et al. (2011) serves to be a comparison of the effects of trauma across cultures. Many psychological phenomena do not carry their effects from one culture to another. In the case of intergenerational trauma, the effects seem to be pronounced in not only the Jewish survivors of the Holocaust but also in the Asian survivors of the Khmer Rouge regime. This finding can be seen as the effect being shown across cultures or as trauma survivors existing as a separate culture unto themselves due to the differences in parenting styles and norms of thought that can be seen as uniquely different between those who have survived such significant large-scale trauma and those of the same culture who have not or have not descended from a survivors.

Myhra, L. L. (2011). It runs in the family: Intergenerational transmission of historical trauma among urban

American Indians and Alaska Natives in culturally specific sobriety maintenance programs. *American Indian & Alaska Native Mental Health Research: The Journal of the National Center, 18*(2), 17-40.

Myhra (2011) examined the effects of trauma upon Native Americans across generations. The trauma that was experienced by Native Americans through forced assimilation and relocations during the nineteenth century correlated to increased levels of alcohol abuse and alcohol dependence. PTSD and substance abuse problems are often co-morbid. The research found that individuals would turn to substance abuse as a maladaptive coping strategy in dealing with the anxiety and depression that resulted from generations of oppression and racism. The racism and oppression served as the traumatic events for past generations. The trauma that past generations experienced was then perpetuated as following generations experienced similar trauma that compounded the effects of the intergenerational transmission. This can be seen as a double trauma for the younger generations.

The article contains a few weaknesses that the author is aware. Primarily, the sample size is small with only thirteen participants. Additionally, there is not a true control group to be able to the findings. The research is more of an ethnographic case study that explores the effects of prior trauma upon the different generations. The research does allow a more personal look into the individual lives of people that have experienced intergenerational trauma. The research also provides a look at how the trauma affects the individuals during childhood, adolescence, and adulthood through a narrative interview.

Gaensbauer, T. J. (2003). Intergenerational transmission of trauma: The infant's experience. *Infant Mental Health Journal, 24*(5), 524-526. doi:10.1002/imhj.10080

Gaensbauer (2003) provides a detailed analysis of Libby who is an infant whose mother suffers from PTSD. The author provides an in-depth look at the connections between the mother's symptoms and Libby's behavior. The author provides three ways that Libby's behavior is affected by the PTSD symptoms. First, he addressed the stress that Libby would be exposed to as a result of the mother having difficulties managing their lives and witnessing the mother's distress caused by her symptoms. Second, her mother defined Libby's definition of fear. Since Libby had not developed a reference of what is considered dangerous in the world, she developed an understanding of what to fear by observing her mother's reactions to the environment, which were abnormal and maladaptive responses. The third manner that Libby was affected by her mother's psychopathology was the result her mother's inconsistent affect regulation and distorted perceptions of reality during interactions between the mother and daughter. The interactions would be pleasant at times, and other times, the interactions seem hostile and anxiety provoking to Libby. The irregularity in mother-daughter bonding could be seen as produce instability in Libby's attachment to her mother that would exacerbate her anxiety and distress.

Gaensbaur (2003) provides detail into the interactions between parent and child in the case of Libby who can be seen as experience intergenerational transmission of trauma. By looking into a single case, the author is able to draw attention to particular facets of the dynamic between the mother and daughter. The details of the particular case can then be compared to other cases of intergenerational trauma to consider possible trends that may have been overlooked in large sample size experiment. The weakness of the article is the possible subjectivity in the author's analysis. The subjectivity is made up for by providing some examples to explain his reasoning. This would allow a critique of the article to provide alternative explanations for the child's behaviors and manifestations of PTSD-like symptoms.

Rowland-Klein, D., & Dunlop, R. (1998). The transmission of trauma across generations: identification with parental trauma in children of

Holocaust survivors. *Australian &*
New Zealand Journal of Psychiatry,
32(3), 358-369.

Rowland-Klein and Dunlop (1998)
interviewed six individuals who were
children of Holocaust survivors to determine
what themes were present across the
individuals that would have contributed to
transmission of trauma across generations.
The research revealed a number of themes
that were consistent across the sample. First,
the sample displayed a number of themes
revolving around their parents' style of
parenting. This theme could be seen in the
comparison of their parents to other parents,
concerns about overprotection, and issues
with separation. The children also heavily

identified with their parent's experiences in a subjective understanding of what the concentration camp experience was like for their parents. An additional finding in the study was that the second generation had showed a heightened state of awareness about the parents' status as being Holocaust survivors through both overt and covert understandings of their parents' story of survival. As a result of these factors, a message of mistrust and fear were transmitted to the second generation through messages about a need to survive in dangerous situations.

The researchers utilized an interview format to conduct the study with a small sample size that consisted of only females, which was a weakness of the study. Despite the weaknesses of the study, the article did present a detailed look at the individual cases and the emerging themes that appeared across the individuals. Additionally, the sample was a non-clinical sample, which serves to be unique because the individuals reported several pathological symptoms associated with PTSD such as hyper-vigilance, mistrust, nightmares, and persistent fears. The article also served to divide the methods of transmission into two categories that include conscious and unconscious transmissions of trauma. In making this distinction between the methods of transmission, Rowland-Klein and Dunlop (1998) present the behaviors of the parents as being a dynamic interaction between the types of forces that magnifies the effect of transmission of trauma across generations.

Iliceto, P., Candilera, G., Funaro, D., Pompili, M., Kaplan, K., & Markus-Kaplan, M. (2011). Hopelessness, Temperament, Anger and Interpersonal Relationships in Holocaust (Shoah) Survivors' Grandchildren. Jour*nal Of Religion & Health, 50*(2), 321-329. doi:10.1007/s10943-009-9301-7

Illiceto et al. (2011) compared the differences between the grandchildren of Holocaust survivors to that of a control group that did not have grandparents who experienced such trauma. The research found that the differences could be found in how the individuals perceived themselves and how they perceived others. The grandchildren of survivors perceived others as being more hostile and rejecting than the control group perceived others to be. They also perceived both themselves and others to be more submissive than the control group. The intergenerational transmission had a deeper impact on the way in which the grandchildren perceived others than themselves. In affecting their perception of others, the trauma influenced the individual's reactions to others. This type of perception of others can be seen to explain the grandchildren's mistrust and hyper vigilance to potential dangers that could be perceived as coming from other individuals.

The research did not explore the

parenting or attachment styles that the individuals experienced as young children or adolescences. This is a shortcoming of the article. If the article were to examine the differences in parenting style to the behaviors presented by the children, the author would have been able to demonstrate how the behaviors were transmitted from parent to child as a result of the trauma. Without examining the potential differences of experiences with-in the groups, the author leaves an opening for the potential of a third variable to explain the differences between the experimental and control group. The article serves to show a correlation between particular outcomes in grandchildren and trauma experienced or not experienced by grandparents. The correlation also contains a weakness as the trauma experienced by the grandparents is only viewed as a dichotomous property as opposed to a continuous property based on the severity of the trauma experienced by the grandparents.

Mellor, ,. J., Davidson, ,. C., & Mellor, D. J. (2001). The adjustment of children of Australian Vietnam veterans: is there evidence for the transgenerational transmission of the effects of war-related trauma?.*Australian & New Zealand Journal Of Psychiatry, 35*(3), 345-351. doi:10.1046/j.1440-1614.2001.00897.x

Mellor, Davidson, and Mellor (2001) examined the differences between children of veteran fathers with PTSD, veteran fathers without PTSD, and civilian fathers. They found that the children of veteran fathers with PTSD displayed higher rates of PTSD symptomology. The two groups whose fathers did not have PTSD showed no difference from each other. In addition, the PTSD group showed lower levels of self-esteem, problem solving, and affective responsiveness. The symptoms of the original PTSD experienced by the father can be seen as having an impact on the attachment between the father and child, which would lead to maladaptive responses to interpersonal interaction. Frustrations that would be experienced when the child would attempt to overcome deficits in affection during a young age could explain the difficulty in problem solving among the children.

The research was well designed by having two groups to compare with the PTSD group. The two control groups serve to answer the possibility of differences between children growing up in a military family and those in a civilian family. The research also explores two facets of intergenerational trauma that has been ignored by many other research articles. First, the article explores the transmission of trauma between the father and the child. Other research has explored the connection between the mother and child but has ignored the possible transmission of trauma by way of the father. The research demonstrates that trauma is also likely to be transmitted from the father to the child also. In addition, the article explores the transmission of wartime trauma that was experienced by an individual who played a role of military personnel who is less of a direct and definable victim than civilians who had been traumatized during wartime events and clearly defined as victims of trauma. In exploring the connection between the father's trauma and the child's manifestation of PTSD like symptoms, the authors make a connection between the child's expression of PTSD and the parent's perceptions as opposed to third party perceptions and expectations.

Sagi-Schwartz, A. (2003). Introduction to the special issue: Extreme life events and catastrophic experiences and the development of attachment across the life span. *Attachment & Human Development, 5*(4), 327-329. doi:10.1080/14616730310001633465

Sagi-Schwartz (2003) explored the effect of trauma upon the parenting ability of the parent in cases of intergenerational trauma. The article posits that mothers who had experienced traumatic events such as the Holocaust, the genocide in Kosovo, rape, or the loss of a loved one lose confidence in their ability to be a safe base for attachment styles that encourage exploration. The author proposes that the trauma decreases the mother's self-esteem and confidence in her parental abilities because of how she was unable to protect herself from such harm. As a result, the child experiences an inadequate relationship with the parent to promote exploration and self-confidence. One can clearly note that the behaviors displayed by the parent are the results of the symptoms of PTSD that are then transmitted to the child. The child then recapitulates the behaviors that are observed and engaged by the parent as being appropriate and normal. This leads to the reactions to trauma being transferred from the parent to the child with the child responding to stimuli in a similar manner as the parent would respond based on the bias created by the traumatic experience.

The article serves to show how the connections between the traumatic event and the child's behavior or perceptions are connected. Sagi-Schwartz (2003) accomplishes this by comparing and contrasting the connections between other research articles and experiments. The article leaves fails to perform a statistical meta-analysis of the associated and supporting work. In doing so, this serves to be a major weakness of the article. The organization of the connections between previous research serves to be a strong point of the article and provides the possibility for continued research into the connections made by the author.

References

Aegidius, K. L., Zwart, J. A., Hagen, K. K., Dyb, G. G., Holmen, T. L., & Stovner, L. J. (2011). Increased headache prevalence in female adolescents and adult women with early menarche. The Head-HUNT Studies. *European Journal Of Neurology, 18*(2), 321-328. doi:10.1111/j.1468-1331.2010.03143.x

Belsky, J., Steinberg, L., Houts, R. M., & Halpern-Felsher, B. L. (2010). The development of reproductive strategy in females: Early maternal harshness → earlier menarche → increased sexual risk taking. *Developmental Psychology, 46*(1), 120-128. doi:10.1037/a0015549

Blair, C., & Raver, C. (2012). Child development in the context of adversity: Experiential canalization of brain and behavior. *American Psychologist, 67*(4), 309-318. doi:10.1037/a0027493

Castel, A. D., Humphreys, K. L., Lee, S. S., Galván, A., McCabe, D. P., & Balota, D. A. (2011). The Development of Memory Efficiency and Value-Directed Remembering Across the Life Span: A

Cross-Sectional Study of Memory and Selectivity. *Developmental Psychology, 47*(6), 1553-1564. doi:10.1037/a0025623

Chen, X. (2012). Culture, peer interaction, and socioemotional development. *Child Development Perspectives, 6*(1), 27-34. doi:10.1111/j.1750-8606.2011.00187.x

Cuevas, K., & Bell, M. (2010). Developmental Progression of Looking and Reaching Performance on the A-Not-B Task. *Developmental Psychology, 46*(5), 1363-1371. doi:10.1037/a0020185

Diesendruck, G., & Markson, L. (2011). Children's assumption of the conventionality of culture. *Child Development Perspectives, 5*(3), 189-195. doi:10.1111/j.1750-8606.2010.00156.x

Doyle, O., McEntee, L., & McNamara, K. (2012). Skills, capabilities and inequalities at school entry in a disadvantaged community. *European Journal Of Psychology Of Education - EJPE (Springer Science & Business Media B.V.), 27*(1), 133-154. doi:10.1007/s10212-011-0072-7

Duncan, G. J., Ziol-Guest, K. M., & Kalil, A. (2010). Early-Childhood Poverty and Adult Attainment, Behavior, and Health. *Child Development, 81*(1), 306-325. doi:10.1111/j.1467-8624.2009.01396.x

Dykas, M. J., & Cassidy, J. (2011). Attachment and the processing of social information across the life span: Theory and evidence. *Psychological Bulletin, 137*(1), 19-46. doi:10.1037/a0021367

Erikson, E. H. (1968). *Identity: Youth and crisis*. New York: Norton.

Garandeau, C. F., Ahn, H., & Rodkin, P. C. (2011). The Social Status of Aggressive Students Across Contexts: The Role of Classroom Status Hierarchy, Academic Achievement, and Grade. *Developmental Psychology*. Advance online publication. doi:10.1037/a0025271

Gupta, R., & Kar, B. (2010). Specific Cognitive Deficits in ADHD: A Diagnostic Concern in Differential Diagnosis. *Journal Of Child & Family Studies, 19*(6), 778-786. doi:10.1007/s10826-010-9369-4

Harden, K., & Mendle, J. (2012). Gene-environment interplay in the association between pubertal timing and delinquency in adolescent girls. *Journal Of Abnormal Psychology, 121*(1), 73-87. doi:10.1037/a0024160

Hohenberger, A., & Peltzer-Karpf, A. (2009). Language learning from the perspective of nonlinear dynamic systems. *Linguistics, 47*(2), 481-511. doi:10.1515/LING.2009.017

Lorber, M. & Egeland, B. (2009) Infancy Parenting and Externalizing Psychopathology from Childhood through Adulthood: Developmental Trends. *Developmental Psychology 45*(4). 909-912. doi: 10.1037/a0015675

Lynch, J. S., van den Broek, P., Kremer, K. E., Kendeou, P., White, M., & Lorch, E. P. (2008). The Development of Narrative Comprehension and Its Relation to Other Early Reading Skills. *Reading Psychology, 29*(4), 327-365. doi:10.1080/02702710802165416

Marchetta, N. J., Hurks, P. M., Krabbendam, L., & Jolles, J. (2008). Interference control, working memory, concept shifting, and verbal fluency in adults with attention-deficit/hyperactivity disorder (ADHD).*Neuropsychology, 22*(1), 74-84. doi:10.1037/0894-4105.22.1.74

Matthews, A., Ellis, A., & Nelson C. (1996). Development of Preterm and Full-Term Infant Ability on AB, Recall Memory, Transparent Barrier Detour, and Means-End Tasks. *Child Development, 67*(6), 2658-2676. doi:10.1111/1467-8624.ep9706244826

Mayeux, L., & Cillessen, A. N. (2008). It's Not Just Being Popular, it's Knowing it, too: The Role of Self-perceptions of Status in the Associations between Peer Status and Aggression. *Social Development, 17*(4), 871-888. doi:10.1111/j.1467-9507.2008.00474.x

McBride Murry, V., Berkel, C., Gaylord-Harden, N. K., Copeland-Linder, N., & Nation, M. (2011). Neighborhood Poverty and Adolescent Development. *Journal Of Research On Adolescence (Blackwell Publishing Limited), 21*(1), 114-128. doi:10.1111/j.1532-7795.2010.00718.x

McKinney, C., & Milone, M. (2012). Parental and Late Adolescent Psychopathology: Mothers May Provide Support When Needed Most. *Child Psychiatry & Human Development, 43*(5), 747-760. doi:10.1007/s10578-012-0293-2

Mendle, J., Leve, L. D., Van Ryzin, M., Natsuaki, M. N., & Ge, X. (2011). Associations between early life stress, child maltreatment, and pubertal development among girls in foster care. *Journal Of Research On Adolescence, 21*(4), 871-880. doi:10.1111/j.1532-7795.2011.00746.x

O'Connor, E., & McCartney, K. (2007). Attachment and cognitive skills: An investigation of mediating mechanisms. *Journal Of Applied Developmental*

Psychology, 28(5/6), 458-476.
doi:10.1016/j.appdev.2007.06.007

Psychogiou, L., Daley, D., Thompson, M. J., & Sonuga-
Barke, E. S. (2008). Parenting empathy: Associations
with dimensions of parent and child
psychopathology. *British Journal Of Developmental
Psychology, 26*(2), 221-232.
doi:10.1348/02615100X238582

Razza, R. A., Martin, A., & Brooks-Gunn, J. (2010).
Associations among family environment, sustained
attention, and school readiness for low-income
children. *Developmental Psychology, 46*(6), 1528-
1542. doi:10.1037/a0020389

Shi, B., & Xie, H. (2012). Socialization of Physical and Social
Aggression in Early Adolescents' Peer Groups: High-
status Peers, Individual Status, and Gender. *Social
Development, 21*(1), 170-194. doi:10.1111/j.1467-
9507.2011.00621.x

United States Department of Health and Human Services.
2012. *2012 HHS Poverty Guidelines.* Retrieved from
http://aspe.hhs.gov/poverty/12poverty.shtml

Van Geert, P. (1998). A Dynamic Systems Model of Basic
Developmental Mechanisms: Piaget, Vygotsky, and
Beyond. *Psychological Review, 105(*4), 634.

Von der Lippe, A., Eilertsen, D., Hartmann, E., & Killen, K. (2010). The role of maternal attachment in children's attachment and cognitive executive functioning: A preliminary study. *Attachment & Human Development, 12(*5), 429-444. doi:10.1080/14616734.2010.501967

Waite, R., & Ramsay, J. (2010). Adults with ADHD: Who Are We Missing?. *Issues In Mental Health Nursing, 31*(10), 670-678. doi:10.3109/01612840.2010.496137

Waszak, F., Hommel, B., & Shu-Chen, L. (2010). The Development of Attentional Networks: Cross-Sectional Findings From a Life Span Sample. *Developmental Psychology, 46*(2), 337-349.

Watanabe, H., Forssman, L., Green, D., Bohlin, G., & von Hofsten, C. (2012). Attention Demands Influence 10- and 12-Month-Old Infants' Perseverative Behavior. *Developmental Psychology, 48*(1), 46-55. doi:10.1037/a0025412

Wierson, M., Long, P. J., & Forehand, R. L. (1993). Toward a new understanding of early menarche: The role of environmental stress in pubertal timing. *Adolescence, 28*(112), 913-924.

www.ingramcontent.com/pod-product-compliance
Lightning Source LLC
Chambersburg PA
CBHW020540290526
45786CB00002B/973